POKÉMON™

HOW TO DRAW

UNOVA HEROES

WRITTEN AND ILLUSTRATED BY RON ZALME

ISBN 978-0-545-36899-5

Published by Scholastic Inc.

12 11 10 9 8 7 6 5 4 3 2 1   11 12 13 14 15 16/0

Designed by Kay Petronio
Printed in the U.S.A.   40
First printing, September 2011

SCHOLASTIC INC.

**New York   Toronto   London   Auckland
Sydney   Mexico City   New Delhi   Hong Kong**

Meet the Pokémon of Unova!

Welcome to the Unova region, where you'll meet lots of never-before-seen Pokémon! Before you start exploring, you'd better know your Pokémon down to the last detail. What better way to get to know them than to draw them? Sharpen your pencil, Trainer . . . your adventures are about to begin!

The Tools

Here's what you'll need to get started —

o Old-fashioned #2 pencils, colored pencils, or mechanical pencils

o Photocopy paper, tracing paper, or newsprint

o A good eraser that doesn't smudge

o Rulers, circle guides, and shaped curves. Using these tools is not cheating! They're necessary to get clean, smooth results.

o Pens, markers, colored pencils, or watercolors to finish your drawings in color

Your Training

You're about to meet fifteen all-new Pokémon. Becoming a Pokémon drawing expert takes time and practice. So don't get discouraged. . . . Keep at it and your drawings will get better and better.

There are four steps to drawing each Pokémon in this book. . . .

Step one: You'll begin each drawing by sketching action lines in black. They're called "action lines" because they show how each Pokémon is moving. Then we'll place several basic shapes in blue to help you build the Pokémon.

Step two: Here you'll add more basic shapes to give your character form.

Step three: Detail time! This is the step that brings out each Pokémon's personality.

Step four: This is your chance to compare your drawing to the original and make adjustments. You can also add shading and color at this stage.

The Shapes

When you draw, you are working with flat, two-dimensional shapes: circles, ovals, squares, rectangles, and triangles. But to make a drawing look believable and exciting, it's important to think in *three* dimensions. You can create depth and volume by using 3-D shapes like spheres, cones, cubes, cylinders, and pyramids.

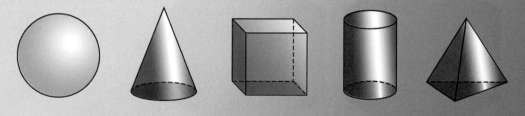

Are you ready? Then turn the page and let's get started!

Snivy

Snivy is one of the three Pokémon new Trainers in Unova receive from Professor Juniper. This clever Grass-type loves the sun — the more sunlight it soaks up, the swifter its movements in battle.

1

Find the two black "action" lines. Notice how each is slightly curved? Sketch them carefully onto your paper. Next, draw the large blue oval for Snivy's body and the smaller one for its head. Use the action lines to help line them up. Finally, add the arm shapes and the foot.

2

Look for the blue lines — these are the new shapes you'll add to your sketch. First, the large curved triangle; next, the eye and mouth. Use another oval to slim down the body and form the tail. Finish with the foot and shoulder.

3

STATS

TYPE: **Grass**
HEIGHT: **2' 00"**
WEIGHT: **17.9 lbs.**

Detail time! Complete the eye and add the lines for Snivy's color pattern. Don't forget the large, three-pronged tail. Check for any missing details.

HINT: Pencils come in various degrees of hard and soft graphite. Hard is great for thin lines, and soft is best for shading.

4

Almost done! Carefully erase your construction lines and darken the lines you're keeping. Compare your drawing to the example, and make corrections. You did it!

Tepig

Tepig is another one of the three Pokémon new Trainers in Unova receive from Professor Juniper. This little Fire-type can blow fire through its nose. If it catches a cold, the fire turns into plumes of black smoke.

1

Start with the two action lines. Find the line that goes across, and then sketch a large circle for the head. Line it up so it just crosses over the line that goes up and down. Next, add the circular body shape.

2

Sketch in ovals for the eye and nose, and half an oval for the mouth. Use the nose to add shape to Tepig's face. Now try the ear, front leg, and the tail circle.

3

Now it's time for the other ear and legs. Once all your basic shapes are in place, move on to the details. Connect the tail circle to the body with a curlicue, and finish the eye and mouth.

Almost done! Use your eraser to remove the unwanted construction lines. Next, darken the lines that are left. If you're happy with your drawing, try finishing it with pen, marker, or even a thin brush with paint or ink.

4

HINT: *Artists often check for symmetry (side-to-side balance) by holding their drawing up to a mirror. How does yours look?*

Oshawott

Oshawott is the third of the three Pokémon Professor Juniper gives to new Trainers in Unova. A Water-type also known as the Sea Otter Pokémon, it is very strong against Fire-types. The scalchop on its stomach can be detached and used as a blade during battle.

1

Draw the action lines lightly, and place the large head circle just above the place where the lines meet. Then sketch smaller crosshairs on the head to help you place Oshawott's features. Add a smaller circle just below the head.

2

Using the small crosshairs as guides, sketch the eyes, nose, and mouth. Pencil in the arm and leg shapes, and then draw the semicircle in the center of Oshawott's stomach.

STATS
◼◼◼

TYPE: **Water**
HEIGHT: **1' 08"**
WEIGHT: **13.0 lbs.**

3

Begin adding your final details, including Oshawott's freckles, toes, ears, and the frills around the collar. Finish the scalchop on the stomach. Don't forget Oshawott's tail!

HINT:

You can shade your drawings with the side of your pencil. Or try dipping your finger into the shavings from your pencil sharpener and using your finger as a crayon!

4

Grab your eraser, clean up your drawing, and finish it with bolder lines. Oshawatt is ready for battle!

Alomomola

Alomomola are covered in a special healing substance. They have been known to assist injured Pokémon they find in the sea and bring them safely to shore.

1

Start with the usual crossed action lines. Then place the two large semicircles. Add another line to the right of where the action lines cross. You'll use this to place Alomomola's features.

2

Following the curve of the action lines, draw the top fin, and then the bottom. It's okay to turn your paper to make it easier. Shorten the body at the end. Next, draw the side fin, eye, and mouth.

STATS
▰ ▰ ▰

TYPE: Water
HEIGHT: 3′ 11″
WEIGHT: 69.7 lbs.

3

Concentrate on the details now. Pencil in elements of the eye; shorten the nose; add lines to the fins . . . you're almost there!

HINT: Many artists like to use layers of tracing paper for each step of their sketches. It saves time erasing later, plus there's less chance of smudging.

4

Compare your drawing it to the original. If it looks good, erase your sketch lines and strengthen the lines you need to keep. Don't forget to add color!

Axew

Axew often marks trees with its strong, sharp tusks. If a tusk breaks, a new one quickly grows in to replace it. This fierce Dragon-type also uses its tusks to crush the berries it eats.

1

Draw the action lines and place the large oval for the head. Then add the crosshairs; you'll use them later to draw the features. Put another oval below the first – this will become Axew's body.

2

Draw the large triangular fin on the back of the head, and then form the eye shape, mouth, and tusks. Finish with the arms and legs.

STATS
◧ ◧ ◧
TYPE: Dragon
HEIGHT: 2' 00"
WEIGHT: 39.7 lbs.

3

Sharpen your pencil . . . it's time to add the fine details! Draw the pupil of the eye, the shape around the neck, the feet and fingers, and a stub of a tail. What other details do you see?

4

Clean up your sketch lines and darken the lines you want to keep. Make corrections, and think about color. Have you tried painting with a brush yet?

HINT: You don't need to buy special shapes to help with your drawings. Instead, collect objects from around the house and use their shapes to draw with. Try buttons, coins, cookie-cutters, paperclips, even flexible wire!

Darmanitan

Darmanitan is a fierce fighter. If it grows weak during battle, it becomes hard and stiff like a statue. Then it uses its psychic powers to fight on. Its internal fire burns at 2,500° F. That's one red-hot Pokémon!

1

To create Darmanitan, you'll need three action lines. Draw the large body circle and use the two sweeping action lines to complete the arms.

2

Add the large eyebrow shapes – use simple arches. Now pencil in the mouth and the circle and oval for the eyes. Sketch the fur on the arms, and then draw the back leg and tail.

STATS
▪▪▪
TYPE: *Fire*
HEIGHT: *4' 03"*
WEIGHT: *204.8 lbs.*

3

Call in the detail squad! Add some lines to the eyebrows. Draw pupils inside the eyes, and add the jagged teeth and some fingers and toes. Don't forget the three circles on Darmanitan's chest!

HINT: Avoid wrinkling your paper as you erase! Artists often use an eraser shield — a flat metal or plastic tool with different cutouts that allow them to erase precisely.

4

Use your eraser to clean away your construction lines, and darken the lines that best suit Darmanitan. Congratulations — you've just completed a very tough Pokémon!

Deerling

Deerling changes color with the turning of the seasons. Its Spring Form is bright pink; its Summer Form is green; its Autumn Form is orange; and its Winter Form is brown.

1

Start with the action lines. Place the head oval near the top. Line up a second oval where the lines cross. Then add the curved line from the oval to the right side of the line.

2

Connect the head to the body. Next, add the eye, nose, and ears. Then draw the left front and rear legs. Finish by adding the tail.

STATS
◪◪◪
TYPE: *Normal-Grass*
HEIGHT: *2' 00"*
WEIGHT: *43.0 lbs.*

3

Copy the legs you drew in the last step to form Deerling's front and rear legs. Now sketch in the flower on top of the head, and finish the eye and nose. Don't forget Deerling's color pattern.

HINT: People once used white correction pens for things written on typewriters. Now they're a great tool for artists — for corrections, or just for drawing in white!

4

Clean up your drawing and start coloring! You've got four different color choices: pink, green, orange, and brown. Why not try them all?

Munna

Munna eats the dreams of both people and Pokémon. When it eats a good dream, it lets out a pink-colored mist. People whose dreams are consumed by Munna forget what they dreamed about.

1

Start with action lines and basic circles . . . you know the routine! The smaller circle is for Munna's head.

2

Use large curves to connect the two circles. This will give Munna's figure some volume. Next, place the two ovals along the horizontal line. The one on the right is an eye. To make the mouth, start at the edge of the head circle and draw toward the crisscross, then loop down and around.

STATS
▾▾▾
TYPE: *Psychic*
HEIGHT: *2' 00"*
WEIGHT: *51.4 lbs.*

3 Add the short triangle shapes that form Munna's feet. Next, add the eyelashes and the patterns on its back.

4 Erase your unwanted sketch lines, and then darken the lines you want to keep. Do you see how all the things you want to draw can be broken down into simple shapes?

HINT: *Take one of your drawings, turn it over, and blacken the back of the paper with the side of your pencil. Place it over a clean sheet and trace the drawing. Instant copy!*

Pansage

This Pokémon lives deep in the forest. It will share the leaves on its head with tired Pokémon. These leaves are known to relieve stress and whisk away weariness.

1

Sketch your action lines, draw the large head oval, and add the two crosshairs. Now draw the slender rectangle to form the body. Finish this step by adding two same-size ovals for Pansage's paws.

2

Draw the two large ears on either side of the head, then fill in the features on Pansage's face. Connect the hands to the body. Notice how the bottom of each arm is a curve, but the top is two angled lines? Sketch in the legs and add an oval off to the side for a tail.

STATS

TYPE: *Grass*
HEIGHT: *2' 00"*
WEIGHT: *23.1 lbs.*

3

Start with the larger shapes, like the leaves on top of Pansage's head. Then do the details – dark pupils, nose, tongue, and inner ears. Don't forget to connect the tail tip to the body.

HINT: Some artists like their brushes very clean and shampoo the bristles. Others think that leaving a bit of paint at the base of the bristles helps keep it pointed. Experiment and decide what works best for you.

4

Clean up your work. Round off your figure lines as you strengthen them - if they're too straight, your figure won't look natural. You're done!

Pidove

Pidove doesn't mind a crowd. It lives in the city and often gathers in flocks in big public areas, like parks and plazas.

1

Place a simple circle and oval along the action lines. These will become Pidove's head and body.

2

Draw a large half oval to form Pidove's chest. The oval from Step One gives the wing volume. Use its position to draw the neck, back, and tail, and then move on to the foot, eye, beak, and the beginning of the raised wing.

STATS
▪▪▪
TYPE: *Normal-Flying*
HEIGHT: *1' 00"*
WEIGHT: *4.6 lbs.*

3

Start by drawing the loops that form the raised wing. Next, add the crest to the head and the other foot. Now it's detail time! Complete the eye, nose, and wing bands.

HINT: *A small fishing tackle box makes a great art kit! The little slots for hooks and lures are perfect for erasers and pencil sharpeners.*

4

Do your usual clean-up, and you've got another Pokémon ready to add to your drawing Pokédex!

Sandile

Sandile moves along below the sand's surface, with only its nose and eyes aboveground. A dark membrane shields its eyes from the sun, and the warm sands prevent its body temperature from dropping.

1

Sketch your two action lines, then place the head circle. Use a thinner oval to define Sandile's eye. Shape the body, then look for the circle of Sandile's belly and draw the wavy line to form its lower body and tail.

2

Start with the oval that will become the tip of Sandile's nose. Then move on to the snout, mouth, and second eye oval. Use a large half oval to form the eye socket. Look at the leg shapes carefully, and then copy them onto your sketch.

STATS
◪ ◪ ◪
TYPE: *Ground-Dark*
HEIGHT: *2' 04"*
WEIGHT: *33.5 lbs.*

3

Add another smaller oval to complete the nose, then finish off the eye socket. Finish drawing the lower jaw, then add the two sharp fangs. Sketch in the right foreleg – you're almost done!

4

Fill in the goggle pattern around Sandile's eyes, then grab your eraser and clean up! Finish the drawing in bold lines and color.

HINT: **Try placing a texture, like canvas or sandpaper, under your paper. Then rub the paper with the side of your pencil, and you can transfer the texture to your artwork!**

Sewaddle

This Grass-type makes clothes for itself.
It chews up leaves and sews them with the
sticky thread that comes from its mouth.

1

Sketch in the action lines,
and then place the large
head circle. Draw the curved
crosshairs over the circle;
next, add a loose oval for the
body. The oval should attach to
the horizontal action line, not
the circle's edge.

2

With the crosshairs
as a guide, center the nose.
Draw Sewaddle's eyes and the
two knobs on top of its head.
Now sketch the triangular
frill from the horizontal action
line. Use same-size circles
for all six legs.

STATS
▾▾▾
TYPE: Bug-Grass
HEIGHT: 1' 00"
WEIGHT: 5.5 lbs.

3

Copy the shapes you see on the frill. Complete the detail for the nose and eyes, and then adjust the side of the face. Finish with the color pattern lines.

HINT: Make a string compass. Get a short piece of string and make a small loop on one end. Put a pencil through the loop and hold the other end of the string with your thumb. Keep the string tight and draw — the string will force your pencil in a smooth circle!

4

Clean up your drawing as you usually would, and then remove the lines from the frill and nose. This will change their shape. Sometimes an artist has to think in terms of "negative" shapes — that is, what's *not* there as well as what's there!

Minccino

Minccino are tidy creatures that love to clean and groom. They greet others of their kind by brushing their tails together. They also use their tails as brooms.

1

Sketch the action lines and place the head shape – it's almost a perfect circle. Put the crosshairs on the head, and then draw a square with rounded corners for Minccino's body.

2

It's time for Minccino's huge ears. Check your sizing; the ears should be larger than its head! Draw the eyes and mouth, and then add the arms and legs.

STATS
▰▰▰
TYPE: *Normal*
HEIGHT: *1' 04"*
WEIGHT: *12.8 lbs.*

3

Bring on the details: the tufts of fur on Minccino's head and chest, and its paws and toes. Finish with the long, sweeping tail.

Do your usual clean-up . . . erase some lines, darken others. Now might be a good time to try a coloring technique you haven't used before. Watercolors, anyone?

4

HINT: TV and movie animators often sketch in light blue and then darken their work with black. The color contrast makes it easier to see mistakes and correct them.

Zoroark

Zoroark live in packs — they bond strongly with others of their kind. They are experts at tricking their opponents with illusions. Each Zoroark can fool a large group of people at once.

1

Zoroark is one of the most challenging Pokémon to draw. You'll need to start with three action lines. Copy the lines shown here, and place the large circle over them. Add a cylinder for the leg, and then the muzzle shape.

2

Starting at the muzzle, add a large ear, mouth, and eye. Sketch the long, flowing mane, and then pencil in the hands and claws. Continue with the legs and feet. Remember to check your sizing.

STATS
◢◢◢
TYPE: *Dark*
HEIGHT: *5' 03"*
WEIGHT: *178.8 lbs.*

3

Time to add the finer details! Carefully draw the features: eye, ear, tongue, and teeth. Sketch in the tufts of fur on the mane, arms, and waist. Stay loose and think fluff! Finish with the end of Zoroark's mane.

4

Don't grab that eraser yet ... there's still more to do! This step shows you how to create the color patterns on Zoroark's mane, eyes, nose, and mouth. Sketch them in and then erase.

HINT: Many illustrations are done by teams of artists. Why not take turns doing these steps with a friend and see how the drawing style changes?

Woobat

Woobat lives in dark forests and caves. It sleeps in caves, hanging from its nose, which uses suction to stick to cave walls. It leaves a heart-shaped mark behind.

STATS
◼◼◼
TYPE: Psychic-Flying
HEIGHT: 1' 04"
WEIGHT: 4.6 lbs.

1 It may look complex, but Woobat is actually pretty simple. Draw the action lines, make a very large circle, and add two simple wing shapes.

2 Complete the wings, and then add the nose shape with a heart inside. The mouth has one triangular tooth.

3 To draw Woobat's fur, follow the outline of the circle. Don't worry about being too exact ...just capture the feel of the fur as you follow the circle's edge.

4 Clean-up time! Erase as you would normally, then ink or color your drawing with your favorite technique. How would you draw the ultrasonic waves Woobat uses?

BRAVO!! You've captured many of Unova's most exciting new Pokémon on paper. But there's plenty more to be found! Pick any Pokémon you like, apply the basic drawing rules you learned here, and your drawing Pokédex will be bursting in no time!